MW01164929

LET'S BREAK UP THE STRESS

# POSITIVE THINKING

## FEEL THE POWER AND ACHIEVE THE IMPOSSIBLE

### (INSPIRATIONAL, MOTIVATIONAL & MORAL SHORT STORIES)

**(N.PAUL)**

## ABOUT THE BOOK

Stress is an ever present in today's madcap and hectic world. It can arrive in a whirlwind, or creep up on us unexpectedly. But however it arrives you can be sure that it brings a set of challenges with it.

Now you can feel the power and achieve the impossible with Let's Break up the Stress: Positive Thinking, which examines the root of s6tress through chapters which include things like;

- Learning how to make beautiful choices
- Keeping wisdom and patience
- Achieving peace of mind
- Attaining greater strength
- Getting to know people before judging them
- Solutions to common problems

With more than 30 short stories, each of them containing inspirational, motivational and moral outlines, you can truly break the pattern of stress in your life and find the answers which will bring you the happiness and success you deserve.

# Table of Contents

## 1. Learn To Make Beautiful Choices

**Jan** asked his Master, "My mind is fluttery always and unclear, what could be wrong with me?"

The Master said, "In order to answer your question, go through the rose garden next to our place and pick the one rose you like the most. But there is a rule. As you pass through the garden, you cannot turn back. You must pick the rose as you go forward only."

Jan went to the Rose garden. As he walked through, He found a rose - fragrant and fully bloomed in the moon light, he instantly liked it but he wondered that he may find a much better one further. So, he walked further, and he saw another rose. But again, he thought the same. When he reached the end of the garden, he couldn't see any rose at all, there were plants which were yet to bear any flowers and he started to regret his decision of letting them all go earlier.

Finally, he gave up. He went back to the Master empty handed.

The Master told him, "You did like the first rose very much but still you kept looking for a better one. And later you realized that what you let go was the best one you could find there. That my dear is called Greed. Greed is a bottomless pit which exhausts the person in an endless effort to satisfy the need without ever reaching satisfaction"

"A bird in hand, is any day worth two in a bush"

## 2. Keep Wisdom and Patience

There was a farmer in Africa who was happy and content. One day a wise man came to him and told him about the glory of diamonds and the power that goes along with them. The wise man said, "If you had a diamond the size of your thumb, you could have your own city. If you had a diamond the size of your fist, you could probably own your own country." And then he went away. That night the farmer couldn't sleep. He was unhappy and he was discontent.

The next morning he made arrangements to sell off his farm and went in search of diamonds. He looked all over Africa and couldn't find any. He looked all through Europe and couldn't find any. When he got to Spain, he was emotionally, physically and financially broke. He got so disheartened that he threw himself into the Barcelona River and committed suicide.

Back home, the person who had bought his farm was watering the camels at a stream that ran through the farm.

Across the stream, the rays of the morning sun hit a stone and made it sparkle like a rainbow. He thought it would look good on the mantel piece. He picked up the stone and put it in the living room. That afternoon the wise man came and saw the stone sparkling. He asked, "Is the farmer back?" The new owner said, "No, why do you ask?" The wise man said, "Because that is a diamond. I recognize one when I see one" .The man said, no, that's just a stone I picked up from the stream. Come, I'll show you. There are many more. They found that the farm was indeed covered with acres and acres of diamonds.

Each of us is, at this very moment is standing in the middle of our own acres of diamonds. If we had only had the wisdom and patience to intelligently and effectively explore the work in which we're now engaged, to explore ourselves, we would most likely find the riches we seek. We fail to recognize the wealth in our own backyard and we end up walking over untold riches every day!!

# 3. Peace of Mind

Once a master was walking from one town to another town with a few of his followers. While they were traveling, they happened to pass a lake. They stopped there and the master told one of his disciples "I am thirsty. Do get me some water from that lake there."

The disciple walked up to the lake. When he reached it, he noticed that some people were washing clothes in the water and, right at that moment, a bullock cart started crossing through the lake. As a result, the water became very muddy, very turbid. The disciple thought, "How can I give this muddy water to my master to drink!" So he came back and told, "The water in there is very muddy. I don't think it is fit to drink."

After about half an hour, the Master asked the same disciple to go back to the lake and get him some water to drink. The disciple obediently went back to the lake. This time he found that the lake had absolutely clear water in it. The mud had settled down and the water above it looked fit to be had. So he collected some water in a pot and brought it to the Master.

The Master looked at the water, and then he looked up at the disciple and said, "See what you did to make the water clean. You let it be ... and the mud settled down on its own, and you got clear water! Your mind is also like that. When it is disturbed, just let it be... Give it a little time. It will settle down on its own. You don't have to put in any effort to calm it down. It will happen. It is effortless."

Having 'peace of mind' is not a strenuous job; it is an effortless process. Just give your mind some time to settle down and there will be peace within soon .When there is peace inside you, it permeates to the outside...

## 4. Call for Greater Strength

A young boy and his father were walking along a forest path. At some point, they came across a large tree branch on the ground in front of them.

The boy asked his father, "If I try, do you think I could move that branch?" His father replied, "I am sure you can, if you use all your strength."

The boy tried his best to lift or push the branch, but he was not strong enough and he couldn't move it.

He said, with disappointment, "You were wrong, dad. I can't move it." "Try again," replied his father.

Again, the boy tried hard to push the branch. He struggled but it did not move. "Dad, I cannot do it," said the boy.

Finally his father said, "Son, I advised you to use all your strength. You didn't. "You didn't ask for my help."

Our real strength lies not in independence, but in interdependence. No individual person has all the strengths, all the resources and all the stamina required for the complete blossoming of their vision. That requires the inspired collaboration of many like-hearted beings. To ask for help and support when we need it is not a sign of weakness, it is a sign of wisdom. It is a wise call for the greater strength that lives in our togetherness.

## 5. Know People before Judging Them

A 24 year old boy and his old aged father were travelling in a train. There was a newlywed couple travelling with him in their compartment. Ten minutes after the onset of journey, looking out from the train's window the 24 year shouted...

"Dad, look the trees are going behind!"

Dad smiled and the young couple sitting nearby, looked at the 24 year Old's childish behavior with pity, suddenly he again exclaimed...

"Dad, look the clouds are running with us!"

The old man smiled at his son again and nodded in affirmation.

The couple couldn't resist and whispered to the old man..."Why don't you take your son to a good doctor? " The old man smiled and said..."I did and we are just coming from the hospital, my son was blind from birth, he just got his eyes last week. For those beautiful things he missed in his childhood due to his blindness, let him hold on to his views for a while". Looks are always deceptive. Every single person on the planet has a story. Don't judge people before you truly know them. The truth might surprise you!!!

## 6. Most Problems have Solutions

Many years ago in a small Indian village, a farmer had the misfortune of owing a large sum of money to a village moneylender. The moneylender, who was old and ugly, fancied the farmer's beautiful daughter. So he proposed a bargain. He said he would forgo the farmer's debt if he could marry his daughter.

Both the farmer and his daughter were horrified by the proposal. So the cunning moneylender suggested that they let providence decide the matter. He told them that he would put a black pebble and a white pebble into an empty money bag. Then the girl would have to pick one pebble from the bag.

If she picked the black pebble, she would become his wife and her father's debt would be forgiven. If she picked the white pebble she need not marry him and her father's debt would still be forgiven. If she refused to pick a pebble, her father would be thrown into jail.

They were standing on a pebble strewn path in the farmer's field. As they talked, the moneylender bent over to pick up two pebbles. As he picked them up, the sharp-eyed girl noticed that he had picked up two black pebbles and put them into the bag. He then asked the girl to pick a pebble from the bag.

The girl put her hand into the moneybag and drew out a pebble. Without looking at it, she fumbled and let it fall onto the pebble-strewn path where it immediately became lost among all the other pebbles.

"Oh, how clumsy of me!" she said. "But never mind, if you look into the bag for the one that is left, you will be able to tell which pebble I picked."

The moneylender dared not admit his dishonesty and the girl walked with pride relieving her father off his debt. The girl changed what seemed an impossible situation into an extremely advantageous one.

Most Problems have Solutions. We just need to think differently.

## 7. Efforts Become Fruitful when we sharpen ourselves

Once upon a time, a very strong woodcutter asked for a job in a timber merchant and he got it. The pay was really good and so was the work condition. For those reasons, the woodcutter was determined to do his best.

His boss gave him an axe and showed him the area where he supposed to work.

The first day, the woodcutter brought 18 trees.

"Congratulations," the boss said. "Go on that way!"

Very motivated by the boss words, the woodcutter tried harder the next day, but he could only bring 15 trees. The third day he tried even harder, but he could only bring 10 trees. Day after day he was bringing less and less trees.

"I must be losing my strength", the woodcutter thought. He went to the boss and apologized, saying that he could not understand what was going on.

"When was the last time you sharpened your axe?" the boss asked.

"Sharpen? I had no time to sharpen my axe. I have been very busy trying to cut trees..."

We sometimes get so busy with our work that we don't take time to sharpen the "axe". In today's world, it seems that everyone is busier than ever, but we should make time to sharpen ourselves, our skills so that our hard work and efforts become fruitful.

## 8. <u>The Right Approach</u>

It once happened, on a certain day, a bull and a pheasant were grazing on the field. The bull was grazing on the grass, the pheasant was picking ticks off the bull; they are partners, you know?

Then the pheasant looked at a huge tree which was at the edge of the field, and very nostalgically said, "Alas, there was a time when I could fly to the top most branch of the tree, but today I do not have the strength even to fly to the first branch of the tree"

The bull very nonchalantly said, "That's no problem! Eat a little bit of my dung every day, you will see, within a fortnight's time you will reach the top of the tree."

The pheasant said, "Oh, come off it! How is that possible?"

The bull replied, "Really, please try and see. The whole humanity is on it, you could try, too."

Very hesitantly, the pheasant started pecking at the dung, and on the very first day it reached the first branch of the tree. In a fortnight's time, it reached the topmost branch Of the tree. After all it required just the strength to make up his mind, to climb the tree and the bull did the trick. The Pheasant just went and sat on the topmost branch and just enjoyed the scenery. The old farmer saw a fat old pheasant on the top of the tree. He took out his shotgun and shot him off the tree.

Any trick can get you to the top, but never lets you stay there. It requires unprecedented efforts to get to the top but clarity and the right approach alone can help you stay there.

## 9. <u>How Do You Handle Adversity?</u>

A young woman went to her mother and told her about her life and how things were so hard for her. She did not know how she was going to make it and wanted to give up. She was tired of fighting and struggling. It seemed as when one problem was solved, a new one arose.

Her mother took her to the kitchen. She filled three pots with water and placed each on a high fire. Soon the pots came to boil. In the first she placed carrots, in the second she placed eggs, and in the last she placed ground coffee beans.

She let them sit and boil; without saying a word. In about twenty minutes she turned off the burners. She fished the carrots out and placed them in a bowl. She pulled the eggs out and placed them in a bowl. Then she ladled the coffee out and placed it in a bowl. Turning to her daughter, she asked, "Tell me what you see."

"Carrots, eggs, and coffee," she replied.

Her mother brought her closer and asked her to feel the carrots. She did and noted that they were soft. The mother then asked the daughter to take an egg and break it. After pulling off the shell, she observed the hard-boiled egg. Finally, the mother asked the daughter to sip the coffee. The daughter smiled as she tasted its rich aroma. The daughter then asked, "What does it mean, mother?"

Her mother explained that each of these objects had faced the same adversity: boiling water. Each reacted differently. The carrot went in strong, hard, and unrelenting. However, after being subjected to the boiling water, it softened and became weak.

The egg had been fragile. Its thin outer shell had protected its liquid interior, but after sitting through the boiling water, its inside became hardened.

However, the ground coffee beans were unique. After they were in the boiling water, they had changed the water. "Which are you?" she asked her daughter.

When adversity knocks on your door, how do you respond? Are you a carrot, an egg, or a coffee bean?

Am I the carrot that seems strong, but with pain and adversity do I wilt and become soft and lose my strength?

Am I the egg that starts with a malleable heart, but changes with the heat? Did I have a fluid spirit, but after a death, a breakup, a financial hardship or some other trial, have I become hardened and stiff? Does my shell look the same, but on the inside am I bitter and tough with a stiff spirit and hardened heart?

Or am I like the coffee bean? The bean actually changes the hot water, the very circumstance that brings the pain. When the water gets hot, it releases the fragrance and flavor.

If you are like the bean, when things are at their worst, you get better and change the situation around you. When the hour is the darkest and trials are their greatest do you elevate yourself to another level?

How do you handle adversity? Are you a carrot, an egg or a coffee bean?

## 10. Don't forget to smile!

A little girl walked to and from school daily. Though the weather that morning was questionable and clouds were forming, she made her daily trek to the elementary school. As the afternoon progressed, the winds whipped up, along with thunder and lightning.

The mother of the little girl felt concerned that her daughter would be frightened as she walked home from school and she herself feared that the electrical storm might harm her child.

Following the roar of thunder, lightning, like a flaming word, would cut through the sky full of concern; the mother quickly got into her car and drove along the route to her child's school.

As she did so, she saw her little girl walking along, but at each flash of lightning, the child would stop, look up and smile.

Another and another were to follow quickly and with each, the little girl would look at the streak of light and smile.

When the mother's car drove up beside the child, she lowered the window and called to her, "What are you doing? Why do you keep stopping?" The child answered, "I am trying to look pretty, and God keeps taking my picture."

Face the storms that come your way and don't forget to smile!

# 11. <u>Blindness, Within Us!</u>

The park bench was deserted as I sat down to read beneath the long, straggly branches of an old willow tree. Disillusioned by life with good reason to frown, for the world was intent on dragging me down.

And if that weren't enough to ruin my day, a young boy out of breath approached me, all tired from play. He stood right before me with his head tilted down and said with great excitement, "Look what I found!"

In his hand was a flower, and what a pitiful sight, with its petals all worn - not enough rain, or too little light. Wanting him to take his dead flower and go off to play, I faked a small smile and then shifted away.

But instead of retreating he sat next to my side and placed the flower to his nose and declared with surprise, "It sure smells pretty and it's beautiful, too. That's why I picked it; here, it's for you."

The weed before me was dying or dead. Not vibrant of colors, orange, yellow or red. But I knew I must take it, or he might never leave. So I reached for the flower, and replied, "Just what I need."

But instead of him placing the flower in my hand, He held it mid-air without reason or plan. It was then that I noticed for the very first time that weed-toting boy could not see: he was blind.

I heard my voice quiver, tears shone like the sun as I thanked him for picking the very best one. "You're welcome," he smiled, and then ran off to play, Unaware of the impact he'd had on my day.

I sat there and wondered how he managed to see a self-pitying woman beneath an old willow tree. How did he know of my self-indulged plight? Perhaps from his heart, he'd been blessed with true sight.

Through the eyes of a blind child, at last I could see the problem was not with the world; the problem was me. And for all of those times I myself had been blind, I vowed to see beauty, and appreciate every second that's mine.

And then I held that wilted flower up to my nose and breathed in the fragrance of a beautiful rose and smiled as that young boy, another weed in his hand about to change the life of an unsuspecting old man.

## 12. Perception: Give Person a Chance to Explain

A teacher teaching Math's to seven-year-old Arnav asked him, "If I give you one apple and one apple and one apple, how many apples will you have?"

Within a few seconds Arnav replied confidently, "Four!"

The dismayed teacher was expecting an effortless correct answer (three). She was disappointed. "Maybe the child did not listen properly," she thought. She repeated, "Arnav, listen carefully. If I give you one apple and one apple and one apple, how many apples will you have?" Arnav had seen the disappointment on his teacher's face. He calculated again on his fingers. But within him he was also searching for the answer that will make the teacher happy. His search for the answer was not for the correct one, but the one that will make his teacher happy. This time hesitatingly he replied, "Four."

The disappointment stayed on the teacher's face. She remembered that Arnav liked strawberries. She thought maybe he doesn't like apples and that is making him loose Focus. This time with an exaggerated excitement and twinkling in her eyes she asked, "If I give you one strawberry and one strawberry and one strawberry, then how many you will have?" Seeing the teacher happy, young Arnav calculated on his fingers again. There was no pressure on him, but a little on the teacher. She wanted her new approach to succeed. With a hesitating smile young Arnav enquired, "Three?"

The teacher now had a victorious smile. Her approach had succeeded. She wanted to congratulate herself. But one last thing remained. Once again she asked him, "Now if I give you one apple and one apple and one more apple how many will you have?" Promptly Arnav answered, "Four!"

The teacher was aghast. "How Arnav, how?" she demanded in a little stern and irritated voice.

In a voice that was low and hesitating young Arnav replied, "Because I already have one apple in my bag."

"When someone gives you an answer that is different from what you expect, don't think they are wrong. There may be an angle that you have not understood at all. You will have to listen and understand, but never listen with a predetermined notion. Most of the times,

We do not try to understand the view of the other person and we find them wrong, but in reality it is just the matter of giving other person a chance to explain."

## 13. Heaven or Hell – Gates are always open!

Once a samurai came to Dzen Master Hakuin and asked: "Where is a paradise? Where is a hell? And where are the gate of heaven and hell?"

Samurai knew only two things: life and death. He did not have any philosophy, he just wanted to know where the gate to escape hell and go to heaven. And Hakuin answered so that the warrior could understand.

"Who are you?" – Hakuin asked.

"I'm the leader of samurai" – the warrior replied – "and the Emperor pays a tribute to me." Hakuin laughed and said: "Are you really the leader of samurais? You look like some poor raga-muffin!"

Samurai's pride was hurt. He forgot why he had come for, whipped out his sword and was going to kill Hakuin.

And Hakuin laughed again and said: "This is the gate of hell. With a sword, being in anger, with your ego you will open it."

Samurai realized that idea, calmed dawn and sheathed his sword. And Hakuin continued: "And here you open the gate of heaven."

Heaven and hell are in you. And the gates are in you. If you are not conscious, this is the gate of hell. If you are vigilant and conscious, this is the gate of heaven. But people continue to think that heaven and hell are somewhere outside. Heaven and hell are not

After life, they are here and now. And the gates are always open. At any moment you make your choice between heaven and hell.

## 14. Life – Full of potholes!

I found myself driving the curvy road near my home slower than usual this morning. My eyes were open as wide as I could get them and I was scanning the road as intently as I could. I was swerving my car to the left and to the right. No, I wasn't drunk, sick, or sleepy. I was just trying to miss all of the potholes. An especially brutal winter had produced a bumper crop of them this year.

As I rounded a curve I saw one that I couldn't miss. I hit it with a jarring thud and in a moment of anger one of those words I try never to use anymore slipped out of my mouth. I shook my head and slowed down even more. As I rounded another curve I saw a man in the road and slowed to a stop. He was directing traffic while his work crew was throwing shovels of asphalt into the worst of the potholes. I smiled at them all and gave them a little wave as I drove on. I knew that their patch job wouldn't last for long but was grateful that it was at least making the road a bit smoother for now.

As we all travel down the road of life we can't help but see that in places it is full of potholes. Pains and problems, difficulties and troubles, challenges and obstacles, sickness and death all lie along that rough road. There is no way to ignore them. There is no way to avoid them. There is no way to travel around them. What we are left with then is a choice. We can curse their existence and rail at God and life or we can take a shovel full of kindness, a shovel full of joy, and a shovel full of love and do our best to fill them in. We can work and pray and have faith that we are making the road a little less rough for those who follow us.

# 15. Today is the Best Day!!

We sat on the swing enjoying the warm summer air, truly without a care in the world. Cody, my 6-year-old nephew laughed, as he swung higher than me. His laugh made me smile.

Afterwards, we went for a walk, looking at the gardens.

As we were walking, Cody looked up at me and said, "Today is the best day!" I smiled at him and replied, "Yes, it is a great day."

I then started thinking about what had we done that day?

We didn't really do anything special; there was nothing that we did that cost any money. It was a simple day - one where we talked, went for walks, and swung on the swing.

So often, we wait for our "best days" without realizing that "today is our best day". Or we say, "When I get this", or, "if only this", or, "when I have more money, I will", and we forget to live every day, enjoying today.

We should be more like children; they truly live in the moment! They don't need expensive things to make them happy; they don't use the phrase, "if only", or, "when I get this", or, "when I have more money". They don't dwell in the past, nor do they worry about the future.

We often hear the expression that we should living in the moment. How do we do that, well watch children as they are the perfect example of living in the moment.

There is a saying, "Carpe Diem" which means, "Seize the Day".

And saying that is full of wisdom, "What I do today is important as I am exchanging a day of my life for It.!" As we get older, we need to remember these sayings and enjoy each and every day.

Keep your child like attitude of "living each moment to its fullest"!

## 16. Excellence is a Function of Practice and Time

A rich man, fond of felines, asked a famous Zen ink painter to draw him a cat. The master agreed and asked the man to come back in three months.

When the man returned, he was put off again and again, until a year had passed.

Finally, at the man's request, the master drew out a brush, and, with grace and ease, in a single fluid motion, drew a picture of a cat – the most marvelous image the man had ever seen.

He was astonished; then he grew angry. "That drawing took you only thirty seconds! Why did you make me wait a year?" he demanded.

Without a word, the master opened up a cabinet, and out fell thousands of drawings of cats.

Excellence is a function of practice and time. Don't rush.

Those of us who are always pushing hard, running up the mountain, may reach the top first only to realize we forgot to enjoy the climb.

Progress takes time. Those who make it look easy have worked hard over time.

## 17. Take what Life has given you-There's no competition in destiny

I was cycling and noticed a person in front of me, about 1/4 of Km. I could tell he was cycling a little slower than me and decided to try to catch him. I had about a km to go on the road before turning off.

So I started cycling faster and faster and every block, I was gaining on him just a little bit. After just a few minutes I was only about 100 yards behind him, so I really picked up the pace and pushed myself. You would have thought I was cycling in the last leg of London Olympic triathlon.

Finally, I caught up with him and passed him by. On the inside I felt so good. "I beat him" of course, but he didn't even know we were racing.

After I passed him, I realized that I had been so focused on competing against him that I had missed my turn, had gone nearly six blocks past it and had to turn around and go all back.

Isn't that what happens in life when we focus on competing with co-workers, neighbors, friends, family, trying to outdo them or trying to prove that we are more successful or more important? We spend our time and energy running after them and we miss out on our own paths to our destinies.

The problem with unhealthy competition is that it's a never ending cycle. There will always be somebody ahead of you, someone with better job, nicer car, more money in the bank, more education, a prettier wife, a more handsome husband, better behaved children, etc.

Take what Life has given you. Stay focused and live a healthy life. There's no competition in destiny. Run your own race and wish others well!!

## 18. A Fair Judgment

Ram and Sham both claimed ownership of the same mango tree.

One day they approached Birbal and asked him to settle the dispute.

Birbal said to them: "There is only one way to settle the matter. Pluck all the fruits on the tree and divide them equally between the two of you. Then cut down the tree and divide the wood".

Ram thought it was a fair judgment and said so.

But Sham was horrified.

"Your Honor" he said to Birbal "I've tended that tree for seven years. I'd rather let Ram have it than see it cut down."

"Your concern for the tree has told me all I wanted to know" said Birbal, and declared Sham the true owner of the tree.

## 19. Change yourself and not the World

Once upon a time, there was a king who ruled a prosperous country. One day, he went for a trip to some distant areas of his country.

When he was back to his palace, he complained that his feet were very painful, because it was the first time that he went for such a long trip, and the road that he went through was very rough and stony. He then ordered his people to cover every road of the entire country with leather. Definitely, this would need thousands of cows' skin, and would cost a huge amount of money.

Then one of his wise servants dared himself to tell the king, "Why do you have to spend that unnecessary" amount of money? Why don't you just cut a little piece of leather to cover your feet?"

The king was surprised, but he later agreed to his suggestion, to make a "shoe" for himself.

To make this world a happy place to live, you need to change yourself and not the world.

## 20. The Anger is within me!!!

A monk decides to meditate alone, away from his monastery. He takes a boat out to the middle of the lake, moors it there, closes his eyes and begins his meditation.

After a few minutes of undisturbed silence, he suddenly feels the bump of another boat colliding with his own. With his eyes closed, he senses his anger rising. Can't the other boatman see that someone is meditating? Reckless fellow! Careless fellow! Insensitive fellow!

He feels the bump again, though this time, it was gentler. After a few minutes...again!

Unable to control himself anymore, he opens his eyes, ready to scream at the boatman who dared disturb his meditation. He sees it's an empty boat that had probably got untethered and floated to the middle of the lake.

At that moment, the monk achieves self-realization. He understands that the anger is within him. It merely needed the bump from an external object to provoke it out of him. From then on, whenever he comes across someone who irritates him or provokes him to anger, he reminds himself, "The other person is merely an empty boat. The anger is within me."

## 21. Don't simply go through Life. Grow through Life

Once there was a King who received a gift of two young eagles from Arabia. They were the most beautiful birds he had ever seen. He gave the precious eagles to his Army General to be trained.

Months passed and one day the Army General informed the King that though one of the eagles was flying high in the sky, the other bird had not moved from its branch since the day it had arrived.

The King summoned bird healers to cure the eagle. But no one could make the eagle fly. Having tried everything else, the King thought, "Maybe I need someone more familiar with the countryside to understand the nature of this problem." So he ordered his Army General, "Go and get a farmer who is familiar with the habits of eagle".

Next day, the King was thrilled to see this lazy eagle soaring high. The King asked the farmer,
"How did you make the eagle fly?" The farmer said to the King, "It was very easy, you're Majesty. I simply cut the branch where the bird was sitting and it had no other option except to fly..."

We are all made to fly. But instead of doing that, we stick to the routine and become lazy. We do only those things which are easy and familiar.

It is very important to analyze the words of William James: "Life isn't about finding yourself, Life is about creating yourself." and also of Henry Ford: "Don't simply go through life. Grow through life." When we accept challenges and targets, a new wave of energy enters us and we get creative and innovative ideas, which make us a different and unique person in the crowd. Then we add new dimension to our life and career.

## 22. No 'Real' Barrier between You and Success!!

During a research experiment a marine biologist placed a shark into a large holding tank and then released several small bait fish into the tank.

As you would expect, the shark quickly swam around the tank, attacked and ate the smaller fish.

The marine biologist then inserted a strong piece of clear fiberglass into the tank, creating two separate partitions. She then put the shark on one side of the fiberglass and a new set of bait fish on the other.

Again, the shark quickly attacked. This time, however, the shark slammed into the fiberglass divider and bounced off. Undeterred, the shark kept repeating this behavior every few minutes to no avail. Meanwhile, the bait fish swam around unharmed in the second partition. Eventually, about an hour into the experiment, the shark gave up.

This experiment was repeated several dozen times over the next few weeks. Each time, the shark got less aggressive and made fewer attempts to attack the bait fish, until eventually the shark got tired of hitting the fiberglass divider and simply stopped attacking altogether.

The marine biologist then removed the fiberglass divider, but the shark didn't attack. The shark was trained to believe a barrier existed between it and the bait fish, so the bait fish swam wherever they wished, free from harm.

Many of us, after experiencing setbacks and failures, emotionally give up and stop trying. Like the shark in the story, we believe that because we were unsuccessful in the past, we will always be unsuccessful. In other words, we continue to see a barrier in our heads, even when no 'real' barrier exists between where we are and where we want to go.

## 23. Time Management

Imagine there is a bank, which credits your account each morning with $ 86, 400, carries over no balance from day to day, allows you to keep no cash balance, and every evening cancels whatever part of the amount you had failed to use during the day.

What would you do? Draw out every pence, of course!

Well, everyone has such a bank. Its name is Time. Every morning, it credits you with 86,400 seconds.

Every night it writes off, as lost, whatever of this you have failed to invest to good purpose.

It carries over no balance. It allows no overdraft. Each day it opens a new account for you.

Each night it burns the records of the day. If you fail to use the day's deposits, the loss is yours. There is no going back. There is no drawing against the "tomorrow."

Therefore, there is never not enough time or too much time. Time management is decided by us alone and nobody else.

It is never the case of us not having enough time to do things, but the case of whether we want to do it.

## 24. You are Special, Don't Ever Forget It!

A well-known speaker started off his seminar by holding up a $20 bill. In the room of 200, he asked, "Who would like this $20 bill?" Hands started going up

He said, "I am going to give this $20 to one of you but first, let me do this."

He proceeded to crumple the dollar bill up. He then asked, "Who still wants it?" Still the hands were up in the air.

"Well" he replied, "what if we do this?" And he dropped it on the ground and started to grind it on the floor with his shoe. He picked it up now, all crumpled and dirty, "now who still wants it?" Still the hands went into the air.

"My friends you all have learned a very valuable lesson. No matter what I did to the money, you still wanted it because it did not decrease in value. It was still worth $20."

Many a times in our life, we are dropped, crumbled and grounded into the dirt by the decisions we make or the circumstances that come our way.

We feel as though we are worthless. But no matter what has happened or what will happen, you will never lose your value. You are special, don't ever forget it!

## 25. We Get Back in Life what we give to others

There was a farmer who sold a pound of butter to the baker. One day the baker decided to weigh the butter to see if he was getting a pound and he found that he was not. This angered him and he took the farmer to court.

The judge asked the farmer if he was using any measure. The farmer replied, amour Honor, I am primitive. I don't have a proper measure, but I do have a scale."

The judge asked, "Then how do you weigh the butter?" The farmer replied "Your Honor, long before the baker started buying butter from me, I have been buying a pound loaf of bread from him. Every day when the baker brings the bread, I put it on the scale and give him the same weight in butter. If anyone is to be blamed, it is the baker."

We get back in life what we give to others.

## 26. Actions Are Never Perfect But Intentions Can Be Pure

Tenali Raman and his wife were going to a friend's wedding. His wife wore her best sari and jewels.

Suddenly from behind, a bullock cart, totally out of control, came rushing by. Tenali quickly pulls his wife towards himself in an effort to bring her to safety, loses balance and both of them fall into a pit along the road.

Wife (upset): "What do you think you were doing? You spoilt my beautiful dress! I can't go to the wedding like this now!"

Tenali: "Well, it's time to buy a new dress then" (as he smiles to himself thanking God that she is safe)!

Have you ever been in situations when you have experienced something unpleasant? Have you noticed that during such times, you end up feeling bad and sometimes even blame someone else?

This is because the awareness that at least the intention was good is not always there. Actions are never perfect but intentions can be pure.

## 27. <u>Words have the Power to Change Reality!!!</u>

There once was a wise sage who wandered the countryside. One day, as he passed near a village, he was approached by a woman who told him of a sick child nearby. She beseeched him to help this child.

So the sage came to the village, and a crowd gathered around him, for such a man was a rare sight. One woman brought the sick child to him, and he said a prayer over her.

"Do you really think your prayer will help her, when medicine has failed?" yelled a man from the crowd.

"You know nothing of such things! You are a stupid fool!" said the sage to the man.

The man became very angry with these words and his face grew hot and red. He was about to say something, or perhaps strike out, when the sage walked over to him and said: "If one word has such power as to make you so angry and hot, may not another have the power to heal?"

And thus, the sage healed two people that day.

"Language does have the power to change reality. Therefore, treat your words as the mighty instruments they are - to heal, to bring into being, to nurture, to cherish, to bless, to forgive." - Daphne Rose Kingma

## 28. Where is your focus in the midst of a storm?

In a forest, a pregnant deer is about to give birth. She finds a remote grass field near a strong-flowing river. This seems a safe place.

Suddenly labour pains begin. At the same moment, dark clouds gather around above and lightning starts a forest fire. She looks to her left and sees a hunter with his bow extended pointing at her. To her right, she spots a hungry lion approaching her.

What can the pregnant deer do? She is in labour! What will happen? Will the deer survive? Will she give birth to a fawn? Will the fawn survive? Or will everything be burnt by the forest fire?

Will she perish to the hunters' arrow? Will she die a horrible death at the hands of the hungry male lion approaching her? She is constrained by the fire on the one side and the flowing river on the other and boxed in by her natural predators.

What does she do? She focuses on giving birth to a new life.

The sequence of events that follows are:

- Lightning strikes and blinds the hunter.

- He releases the arrow which zips past the deer and strikes the hungry lion.

- It starts to rain heavily, and the forest fire is slowly doused by the rain.

- The deer gives birth to a healthy fawn.

In our life too, there are moments of choice when we are confronted on all sides with negative thoughts and possibilities. Some thoughts are so powerful they overcome us and overwhelm us.

Maybe we can learn from the deer. The priority of the deer, in that given moment, was simply to give birth to a baby. The rest was not in her hands, and any action or reaction that changed her focus would have likely resulted in death or disaster.

## 29. Try to Find Positives in your Negatives!!!

A young woman was sitting at her dining table, worried about taxes to be paid, house-work to be done and to top it all, her family was coming over for Thanksgiving the next day. She was not feeling very thankful at that time.

As she turned her gaze sideways, she noticed her young daughter scribbling furiously into her notebook. "My teacher asked us to write a paragraph on "Negative Thanksgiving" for homework today." said the daughter, "She asked us to write down things that we are Thankful for, things that make us feel not so good in the beginning, but turn out to be good after all."

With curiosity, the mother peeked into the book. This is what the daughter had written:

"I'm thankful for Final Exams, because that means school is almost over. I'm thankful for bad-tasting medicine, because it helps me feel better. I'm thankful for waking up to alarm clocks, because it means I'm still alive."

It then dawned on the mother, that she had a lot of things to be thankful for!

She thought again...

She had to pay taxes but that meant she was fortunate to be employed.

She had house-work to do but that meant she had her own home to live in.

She had to cook for her family for Thanksgiving but that meant she had a family with whom she could celebrate.

We generally complain about the negative things in life but we fail to look at the positive side of it. What is the positive in your negatives? Look at the better part of life this day and make it a great day!

## 30. Take Me to My Mother!!!

A man stopped at a flower shop to order some flowers to be wired to his mother who lived two hundred miles away.

As he got out of his car he noticed a young girl sitting on the curb sobbing. He asked her what was wrong and she replied, "I wanted to buy a red rose for my mother. But I only have seventy-five cents, and a rose costs two dollars."

The man smiled and said, "Come on in with me. I'll buy you a rose." He bought the little girl her rose and ordered his own mother's flowers.

As they were leaving he offered the girl a ride home. She said, "Yes, please! You can take me to my mother." She directed him to a cemetery, where she placed the rose on a freshly dug grave.

The man returned to the flower shop, canceled the wire order, picked up a bouquet and drove the two hundred miles to his mother's house.

# 31. Great Power behind Self-Confidence!!!

A Business executive was deep in debt and could not see any way out. Creditors and Suppliers were demanding payments. He sat in the park, wondering if anything could save his company from bankruptcy.

Suddenly an old man appeared before him and asked, "I can see that something is troubling you seriously". After listening to the executive the old man said, "I believe I can help you".

He asked the man his name, wrote out a cheque and put it into his hands saying, "Take this money, meet me here exactly one year from today and you can pay me back at that time". Then he turned and disappeared as quickly as he had come.

The business executive saw in his hands a cheque for $500,000 signed by Warren Buffet, one of the richest men in the world. "I can erase my worries instantly" he realized. But instead, the executive decided to put the uncashed cheque in his safe knowing that it might give him the strength to work out to save his business and to use this only in case of dire emergency. With changed thinking he negotiated better deals, restructured his business and worked rigorously with full zeal and enthusiasm and got several big deals.

Within few months, he was out of debt and started making money once again. Exactly one year later he returned to the park with the uncashed cheque. As agreed, the old man appeared. But just as he was about to hand him back the cheque and share his success story, a nurse came running up and grabbed the old man.

"I'm so glad I caught him" she cried. "I hope he hasn't been bothering you much. He always escapes from the mental hospital and tells people that he is Warren Buffet", saying this she took the old man away.

The surprised executive just stood there, stunned! All year long he had been dealing thinking that he had half a million dollars behind him.

It's not the money, real or imagined that turns our life around. It is our self-confidence that gives us the power to achieve anything we want.

# 32. No One can Replace You!!

A little boy went to his old grandpa and asked, "What's the value of life?" The grandpa gave him one stone and said, "Find out the value of this stone, but don't sell it."

The boy took the stone to an Orange Seller and asked him what its cost would be. The Orange Seller saw the shiny stone and said, "You can take 12 oranges and give me the stone. "The boy apologized and said that the grandpa has asked him not to sell it.

He went ahead and found a vegetable seller. "What could be the value of this stone?" he asked the vegetable seller. The seller saw the shiny stone and said, "Take one sack of potatoes and give me the stone. "The boy again apologized and said he can't sell it.

He then went into a jewelry shop and asked the value of the stone. The jeweler saw the stone under a lens and said, "I'll give you 1 million for this stone." When the boy shook his head, the jeweler said, "Alright, alright, take 2, 24 Karat Gold necklaces, but give me the stone. "The boy explained that he can't sell the stone.

Further ahead, the boy saw a precious stone's shop and asked the seller the value of this stone. When the precious stone's seller saw the big ruby, he lay down a red cloth and put the ruby on it. Then he walked in circles around the ruby and bent down and touched his head in front of the ruby. "From where did you bring this priceless ruby from?" he asked. "Even if I sell the whole world, and my life, I won't be able to purchase this priceless stone."

Stunned and confused, the boy returned to the grandpa and told him what had happened. "Now tell me what the value of life, grandpa is?" Grandpa said, "The answers you got from the Orange Seller, the Vegetable Seller, the Jeweler & the Precious Stone's Seller explain the value of our life. You may be a precious stone, even priceless, but, people will value you based on their financial status, their level of information, their belief in you, and their motive behind entertaining you, their ambition, and their risk taking ability. But don't fear, you will surely find someone who will recognize your true value."

Respect Yourself. Don't Sell Yourself Cheap. You are Rare, Unique, Original and no one can replace YOU.

## 33. Conclusions often skip the Truth!!!

A woman was waiting at an airport one night, with several long hours before her flight. She hunted for a book in the airport shops, bought a bag of cookies and found a place to sit.

While she was engrossed in her book ,a man sitting beside her grabbed a cookie or two from the bag in between, which she tried to ignore to avoid a scene.

So she munched the cookies and watched the clock, as the gutsy cookie thief diminished her stock. She was getting more irritated as the minutes ticked by, thinking, "If I wasn't so nice, I would blacken his eye."

With each cookie she took, he took one too, when only one was left, she wondered what he would do. With a smile on his face, and a nervous laugh, he took the last cookie and broke it in half.

He offered her half, as he ate the other, she snatched it from him and thought... oooh, brother. This guy has some nerve and he's also rude, why he didn't even show any gratitude!

She had never known when she had been so galled, and sighed with relief when her flight was called. She gathered her belongings and headed to the gate, refusing to look back at the thieving ingrate.

She boarded the plane, and sank in her seat, then she sought her book, which was almost complete. As she reached in her baggage, she gasped with surprise, there was her bag of cookies, in front of her eyes.

If mine are here, she moaned in despair, the others belonged to him and he tried to share. Too late to apologize, she realized with grief, that she was the rude one, the ingrate, the thief.

When you jump to conclusions you often skip over the truth and sometimes it is too late to make amends.......

CPSIA information can be obtained
at www.ICGtesting.com
Printed in the USA
BVOW08s1741050217
475350BV00011B/281/P

9 781542 824095